This book belongs
to:

_____

Also by Ashley Rice

*girls rule ...a very special book
created especially for girls
Love Is Me and You
Thanks for Being My Friend
You Are an Amazing Girl*

Library of Congress Control Number: 2004096957
ISBN: 0-88396-832-0

Certain trademarks are used under license.

Printed in the United States of America.
Second Printing: 2006

 This book is printed on recycled paper.

Blue Mountain Arts, Inc.
P.O. Box 4549, Boulder, Colorado 80306

You Go, Girl...
Keep Dreaming

a special book about
always believing in yourself

Ashley Rice

Blue Mountain Press™
Boulder, Colorado

An Introduction
by Penelope J. Miller

Hi! My name is Penelope J. Miller, and I am the narrator of a book called **girls rule** and now this book, too. I'm excited that I get to tell you what this book is about and to make the journey through its pages right alongside you.

The drawings and writings in this book were created to encourage girls like you to follow your dreams and be who you are. It's important to be yourself, believe in yourself, and be the star of your own life. It's also important for you to know that doing anything often involves a lot of messing up. Sometimes I think we don't try things we want to because we are afraid that we won't be immediately successful or perfect. It seems to me the only way you can get where you are going is by jumping over each and every hurdle along the way, even if on the first round you miss each and every one.

When the path to my dreams is a little bumpy, I figure things out by writing my thoughts down (that's why there's a page in here for you to write your thoughts, too). Maybe your way of figuring things out — and your dream — has to do with math or gymnastics or science. Maybe you figure things out about your life by talking to people or by playing soccer. It doesn't matter; the world is full of ideas and each person brings something special to the world that no one else can bring. This is what I say to that whole idea: hang on to your dreams and give your life everything you've got.

So anyway, I hope that wherever you are, you're doing well — and that you always believe in your dreams.

your friend,

Penelope J.

you go, girl :

In this world...
wishing you:
a little peace
a little love
a little luck
a little sunshine
a little happiness
a little fun...

...and as far
as reaching your
dreams
and goals?

...you can do it, girl:
you go.

Keep dreaming!

doctor

sister

artist

princess

friend

goddess

angel

astronaut

daughter

writer

girl

president

Woman

athlete

You can be anything!

girls
who change
the **world**

There are girls who make
things better... simply by showing up.
There are girls who make things happen,
girls who make their way.
There are girls who make a difference,
girls who make us smile.
There are girls who do not make excuses,
girls who cannot be replaced.
There are girls of wit and wisdom, who —
with strength and courage — make
it through.
There are girls who change the world
every day by dreaming and then acting to
accomplish their goals...

girls like you.

You are a rainbow
in the sky

You are an
extra-special
somebody,

you are a
special butterfly.

You are the
favorite flavor
of the bunch...

like double-
chocolate-cherry
pie.

You are
an angel

and a joker,

a mystery
that never lies.

Like a dream
sent to the stars,
you are...

a rainbow in the sky.

Some words about
you:

amazing
wonderful...
electrifying
heartbreaking
cute...
killer-smart
dazzling...
one-of-a-kind...

and you are
one of the great
girls I know...

I believe in you

I believe in the way that you are
and the way you will be.
I believe in the things that you say.
You mean the world to me.
And if you should go,
if you should turn around one day,
if you should ever doubt your dreams
in any way,
don't think twice about it.
Don't worry too long
about whether you'll find a place
for yourself in the world — you belong.

I know that you'll get where
you're going someday.
For no matter what happens,
you will find a way.
I believe in the way that you are
and the way you will be.
You are a Shining Star
in this world...

and you mean the world

to me.

There is one rule and
only one rule
you need
to follow...

as you go through this world...
if you want to make your way
as a star ...

do the **best** you can.

Helpful hint #1:
on getting rid of self-doubt

Self-doubt is a lot
like brain freeze...

your
brain,
cold →

think about something
else...

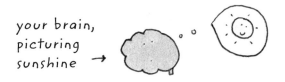

your brain,
picturing
sunshine →

...and it will eventually
go away.

your
brain, →
happy

Always be yourself...
for no one else
can compare to
the integrity of
your own
heart...

The power to be oneself is
perhaps one of the best gifts a person
can both "have" and — at the same
time — give. It is when we are our
true selves that we find our best
friends, write our best lines, and
score the most points 🖊📄
on the never-ending tests
that are eternally placed
before us. It is when we are our
true selves that we discover
things we have in common with
others... ★ ★ ★ by way of an
empathetic smile in response
to something we've just said
or by running into others on
the path that we've chosen...
just because they, too, in being
themselves and following

their hearts' have chosen the same path. It is when we are ourselves that we shine the brightest, laugh the loudest, and learn the most.

Being oneself often includes times we have to run ahead or wait behind....

It's when we are ourselves that we can pass off courage to another person. This, my friend, is the "gift" part and the reason why being oneself is never a selfish act, but one which is rooted — always, always — in love, friendship, and courage.

is a mountain *scaled in courage...*

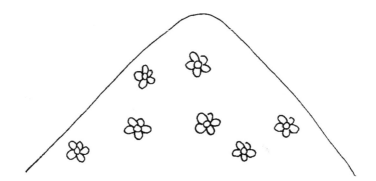

When the task at hand is a mountain
in front of you,
it may seem too hard to climb.
But you don't have to climb it
all at once —
just one step at a time.
Take one small step...
and one small step...
then another...
and you'll find...
the task at hand that was a mountain
in front of you...
is a mountain you have climbed.

Helpful hint #2:
or what the first-ever bird taught the World
★

When the ground falls
out from below you...

learn to fly.

If you have never failed...
then you probably have not been
"fighting" in the right "weight" class —
with the best 😊 😊 😊 competition.
💗 If you have never been hurt...
then you have probably never gone
after something that you loved.
If you have never been frightened...
then you * have probably never put
yourself on the line or cared about
something enough to — win or lose —
simply give it everything you've
got ... you know: give it your all.
If you have never fallen... then
you have not grown or learned how
to get ✦ ✦ 😊 up. If you have never
lost ... then you probably
have not taken enough
chances...

So: if learning and living involve so much "failing" and faltering... how do you know if you're ever doing anything right?...

...because when you fall — you fall; but your heart... it dances.

☆

A little advice:

If you are not sure
which way to go...

ask your heart —
your heart will
Know.

When your mind
does not know
what to say...

your heart will
find a way.

When you can't See
the finish line
or when your dreams
seem hard to find...

Know that you
Know the way:
your heart will
lead you there
one day.

Take these things with you
wherever you go:

friendship   fun ☺

love♡   hope ✿

a belief in your dreams ✦

a belief in your goals...

and a *determination*
    to get **you** <u>wherever</u>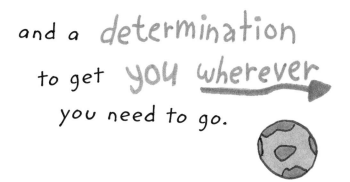
    you need to go.

Things I want to do when I grow up ☺

Things I want to do now:

You are a

girl

who is

1. sharp

2. intelligent

3. amazing

4. brave...

5. remarkable

6. independent

7. incredible

8. daring

You can <u>do</u> anything!

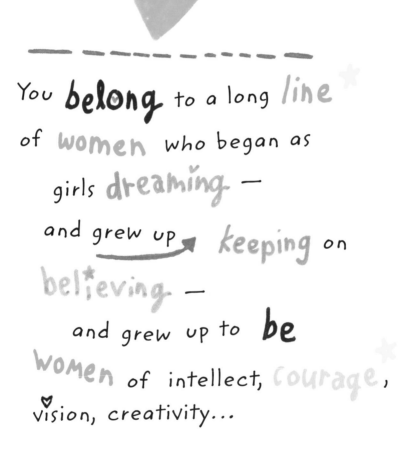

You **belong** to a long *line*
of women who began as
girls dreaming —
and grew up keeping on
believing —
and grew up to **be**
women of intellect, courage,
vision, creativity...

... women who Make
a difference.

And as far as I can tell,
you are well
on your way
to becoming
one such woman.

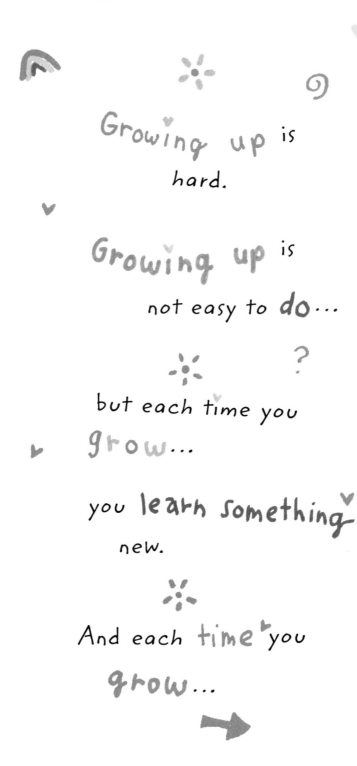

Growing up is
hard.

Growing up is
not easy to do...

but each time you
grow...

you learn something
new.

And each time you
grow...

you get a little bit closer...

to your dreams coming true.

Growing up is not easy to do, but it's worth it.

How to **get** to your
future:

1. **work** hard

2. **Study** hard

3. learn as much as **possible** ...

4. laugh

5. have fun

6. and Make your
   future your own.

Winning your own heart:

Find a little happiness.

Find a little hope.

Find a little or even a very
   big place where you can
   go.

Find a little (or big) but very
   excellent dream.

Find some true and some real
   fun.

If you can do these five
   things...

...you've won.

You are an **incredible** girl.

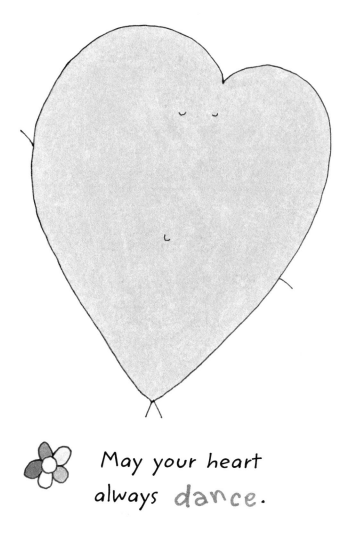

May your heart always **dance**.

Helpful hint #3:

on hope*

You gotta **have** hope
and you gotta keep trying*
and you gotta keep **believing**
that everything you are striving
for and trying to do is worth
something.
You gotta have some* heart*
and you gotta **have** drive...
but mostly you gotta have hope...

...and hope comes
from inside.

If you were a...

If you were
a ⭐ star...

you'd be the
○ bright one.

You'd be the
rare 🌈 rainbow
if rainbows
were 💜 few.

If you were
an answer...

you'd be the
right one.

👟 You'd be
the perfect
fit, if you were
a shoe.

If you were
a fine
pie...   you'd be the
                finest one.

You'd be 😐 nice
    as the 🙂 sunshine
that makes the
    sky blue...

but you're you...
    which is better
than all these
    things put together.

A graceful intellect...

...a true and strong character...

What you've got

a brave sense of wit and humor and knowingness...

the guts to go...

the heart to believe and to live and to dream.

...and style, baby —
style.

If someone were to write
a book about you,
it would be a
book about

a dreamer,
a hoper,
a looker,
a seeker,
an imaginer,
a creator,
a good secret-
    keeper,

a mover,
a shaker,
a magic-dream-
    maker,
an artist,
an angel,
a listener,
a friend.

...and flower power

Daisy power:

A daisy is a very special *flower* that needs

SuNlight,
dreams,
and *goals*
to grow
up STRONG...
and it's clear
to me that
you've got
daisy
power...

'cuz girl, your dreams
are growing by the
hour.

Helpful hint #4:

be free
to
believe
in dreams...

and never
give up.
♡

You are your own best advisor,

your own best judge of your heart...

your own best dream-maker, map-maker, and compass.

You are your own best go-getter and your own best cheerleader when things are going rough.

You are You...

and that's more than enough!

You go, girl —
you fly.

You are
one of the
many girls who
are changing the
world for the better.

Keep on **dancing**. Keep
on **trying**. Keep ♡ @
believing, even after you've
been crying. keep on
daring. Keep on
sharing your *heart*.
Keep on **dreaming**...

And always, **always**,
always, always,
always believe
in your dreams. ♥

Facts about you:

your full name:

- - - - - - - - - - - - - - -

your nicknames:

- - - - - - - - - - - - - - -

your permanent address:

- - - - - - - - - - - - - - -

song you listen to most:

- - - - - - - - - - - - - - -

your favorite book/color/movie:

- - - - - - - - - - - - - - -

where you go when you
    need to go someplace:

... ✓

- - - - - - - - - - - - - - -